MARTIAL ARTS

KARATE

BY ASHLEY STORM

WWW.APEXEDITIONS.COM

Copyright © 2024 by Apex Editions, Mendota Heights, MN 55120. All rights reserved. No part of this book may be reproduced or utilized in any form or by any means without written permission from the publisher.

Apex is distributed by North Star Editions:
sales@northstareditions.com | 888-417-0195

Produced for Apex by Red Line Editorial.

Photographs ©: Kevin Langley/Icon Sportswire/AP Images, cover; iStockphoto, 1, 10–11, 16–17, 19, 29; Shutterstock Images, 4–5, 6–7, 8, 12–13, 18, 20–21, 22–23, 24, 25, 27; US Navy/AP Images, 14; Columbia Pictures/Moviepix/Getty Images, 15

Library of Congress Control Number: 2023910175

ISBN
978-1-63738-765-8 (hardcover)
978-1-63738-808-2 (paperback)
978-1-63738-890-7 (ebook pdf)
978-1-63738-851-8 (hosted ebook)

Printed in the United States of America
Mankato, MN
012024

NOTE TO PARENTS AND EDUCATORS

Apex books are designed to build literacy skills in striving readers. Exciting, high-interest content attracts and holds readers' attention. The text is carefully leveled to allow students to achieve success quickly. Additional features, such as bolded glossary words for difficult terms, help build comprehension.

TABLE OF CONTENTS

CHAPTER 1
STRONG STRIKES 4

CHAPTER 2
KARATE HISTORY 10

CHAPTER 3
LEARNING KARATE 16

CHAPTER 4
COMPETING 22

COMPREHENSION QUESTIONS • 28
GLOSSARY • 30
TO LEARN MORE • 31
ABOUT THE AUTHOR • 31
INDEX • 32

CHAPTER 1

STRONG STRIKES

Two girls take their places on the mat. They bow to the **referee** and to each other. Then the karate match begins.

Many karate matches are split into two or three parts. Each part lasts two or three minutes.

Fighters often raise their arms to block kicks or punches.

One girl kicks. But her **opponent** is ready. She uses her arm to block. Then she takes a deep breath and punches.

FAST FACT

In some matches, fighters hit as hard as they can. This is called full-contact karate.

The first girl tries to block, but she is too late. Her opponent scores a point. Then she gets ready to strike again.

BREAKING BOARDS

Karate strikes can be very powerful. Some kicks and punches can break boards. People use their bare hands and feet. They can snap boards that are 1 inch (2.5 cm) thick.

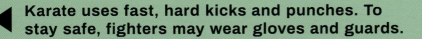

Karate uses fast, hard kicks and punches. To stay safe, fighters may wear gloves and guards.

CHAPTER 2

KARATE HISTORY

Karate comes from Okinawa. This group of islands is in the Pacific Ocean. People there have practiced karate for hundreds of years.

People on Okinawa may have been practicing karate as long ago as the 1300s.

Early forms of karate taught unarmed fighting. People used fists and feet instead of weapons.

In the 1600s, Japan started taking over Okinawa. New styles of karate developed. By the 1920s, they began spreading throughout Japan.

FAST FACT

Japan made carrying swords in Okinawa **illegal**. So, people used karate instead.

US soldiers were sent to Japan during and after World War II (1939–1945).

In the 1940s, US soldiers were **stationed** in Okinawa. They learned karate. They brought it to the United States. Karate also spread to other countries.

THE KARATE KID

Movies and TV shows helped make karate popular. *The Karate Kid* is one example. This movie came out in 1984. It's about a boy who uses karate to stand up to bullies.

The Karate Kid is the first in a series of movies about a boy who learns to fight.

CHAPTER 3

LEARNING KARATE

Today, karate is one of the most popular martial arts. Millions of people around the world study it.

People of all ages can learn karate.

Students often study karate at a school called a dojo.

Most people take classes to learn karate. Students practice many types of kicks, punches, and **stances**. They also learn to block and dodge.

BELT COLORS

Karate students wear colored belts. The color shows each student's skill level. Beginners wear white belts. **Experts** wear black belts. Students must pass tests to advance to higher levels.

Earning a black belt takes years of practice.

People practice doing sets of 20 or more moves in a row.

Students also practice kata. That means doing sets of moves in a row. People memorize the order. They also work to have the right **form** for each move.

FAST FACT

In some moves, people stand with their legs spread wide. This helps them balance.

CHAPTER 4

COMPETING

Some people compete in karate. There are several types of events. In kata events, people perform sets of moves. Judges watch them and give scores.

In kata events, people earn points based on how well they do each move.

In kumite matches, fighters get points for kicks or punches to an opponent's head or upper body.

At kumite events, people fight in pairs. Fighters score points for hits and kicks. The fighter with the most points wins.

SCORING POINTS

In kumite, some moves score one point. Others score two or three. Scores depend on the type of kick or punch. Form and timing matter, too.

Referees and judges watch matches and decide when fighters earn points.

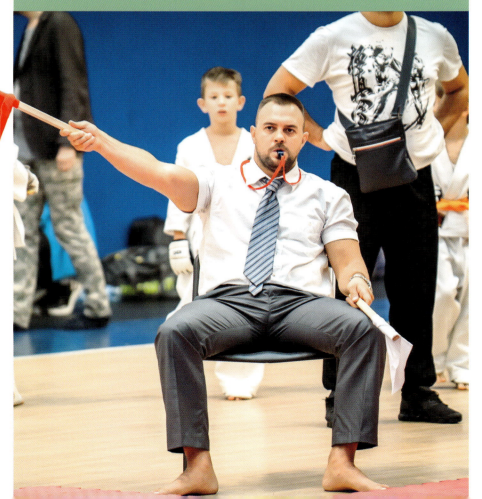

Top fighters go to the World **Championships**. People do kata events there as well. Some compete as **individuals**. Others work together for team events.

FAST FACT

Many karate students do not compete. For them, karate is about keeping their minds and bodies strong.

Ashihara events blend karate with other fighting styles.

COMPREHENSION QUESTIONS

Write your answers on a separate piece of paper.

1. Write a sentence that explains the main idea of Chapter 2.

2. Would you rather compete in a kata event or a kumite event? Why?

3. What belt color does a new karate student wear?
    - **A.** red
    - **B.** white
    - **C.** black

4. Why would karate be useful in a place where swords are illegal?
    - **A.** Karate cannot be used for fighting.
    - **B.** Karate lets people fight without weapons.
    - **C.** Karate helps people hide weapons.

5. What does **developed** mean in this book?

*New styles of karate **developed**. By the 1920s, they began spreading throughout Japan.*

    A. started
    B. ended
    C. called

6. What does **perform** mean in this book?

*In kata events, people **perform** sets of moves. Judges watch them and give scores.*

    A. sing songs or play music
    B. do something in front of others
    C. decide the winner of a contest

Answer key on page 32.

GLOSSARY

championships
The top competitions in a league or sport.

experts
People who are very good at something.

form
The correct way of holding the body while doing a move.

illegal
Against the law.

individuals
People doing things on their own.

opponent
A person who someone is fighting against.

referee
A person who makes sure rules are followed.

stances
Ways of placing the feet and holding the lower body.

stationed
Sent to a place as part of serving in the military.

TO LEARN MORE

BOOKS
Allan, John. *Be the Best at Karate*. Truro, UK: Hungry Tomato, 2022.

Krohn, Frazer Andrew. *MMA: Heroic History*. Minneapolis: Abdo Publishing, 2023.

Vink, Amanda. *Karate*. New York: PowerKids Press, 2020.

ONLINE RESOURCES
Visit **www.apexeditions.com** to find links and resources related to this title.

ABOUT THE AUTHOR
Ashley Storm has written more than 30 books for children and teens. She lives in Kentucky with her husband, three mischievous cats, and a flock of bossy backyard chickens who peck on the door to demand treats. She took karate lessons when she was a kid.

B
belts, 19
block, 7, 9, 18
boards, 9

D
dodge, 18

E
events, 22, 24, 26

J
Japan, 13

K
Karate Kid, The, 15
kata, 21, 22, 26
kick, 7, 9, 18, 24–25
kumite, 24–25

O
Okinawa, 10, 13–14

P
points, 24–25
punch, 7, 9, 18, 25

S
stances, 18
strikes, 9

W
World Championships, 26

ANSWER KEY:
1. Answers will vary; 2. Answers will vary; 3. B; 4. B; 5. A; 6. B